POETIC JOURNEY

Hope-Life-Regret-Love

Tony Gordon

Eargasmic Ink Publishing

Atlanta. Georgia

ISBN -13: 978-0615765518

Cover Photography: Cherelle Scott

Cover Model: Draper Peters

First Edition

Printed in the United States of America

Eargasmic Ink Publishing

Atlanta, Georgia

Dedication

To all the people that I have met along this journey.

Know that your impact was noted.

Acknowledgements

I thank God for blessing me with this gift.

I thank my mom and dad for giving me a sense of humor,

And encouraging me to do great things.

I thank my Stepmother for always believing in me.

I thank my Grandmothers for teaching me to speak my mind.

I thank my Aunts, Uncles, and Cousins for spoiling me.

I thank my brothers and sisters for loving me unconditionally.

I thank my friends for being a part of my team.

I thank Vickie and Dee two friends that always listen to me vent, and offer good advice, even if I am wrong.

I thank Fran for pushing me to finish this project.

And to everyone else that has supported my cause

I appreciate you all.

God Bless

For my Mother, Father, Grandmothers,

Aunts, and Friends, in memory.

Table of Contents

Hope

Life

Regret

Love

POETIC JOURNEY

Hope-Life-Regret-Love

HOPE

This chapter on Hope was inspired by the poem "Encouragement". A person can go weeks without food, days without water, but is less likely to last 24 hours without hope. An image of hope makes a world of difference to a person whose spirit is down and out. As the poem states, "Don't be afraid to reach for the stars, and don't be afraid to dream beyond Mars". This is simply encouraging a person to dream, and when you dream you have hope. In dreaming you have to dare to trust the things you can't see, and then you will be amazed at what you can be. Along with your dreams comes a test of life, and it may seem hard to pass, but if you trust in hope, success will come at last. Understand that in pursuing your dreams things may get rough, but if you adhere to hope, you can see your dreams manifest before you. In my decades of living I have found it vital that I inspire others with hope. There are several words that complement the word hope: (Encouragement, Inspire, Uplift, and Revive) These words used in combination with hope makes for a great recipe for success. It is my hope that this section inspires someone to start dreaming and reaching for the stars. After all, you'll be amazed at what you can be.

A Moment In Time

A timeless pleasure is what you are

A moment in time by far.

The nicest thing I ever imagined

Puff, puff, puff goes your magic

Dragon.

You really should be a superstar

In my eyes you already are.

A perfect image of what hope should be

A moment in time in front of me.

Keep hope alive and you'll never

Fail.

In the end the timeless pleasure will

Prevail.

Keep Rising...

A Stray Child

Somewhere out there is a stray child with no place to call his own.

He spends the majority of his time wishing that he was grown.

A seed sowed into this earth

who didn't stand a chance, even from

Birth.

A child as helpless as can be

has

no ties to his family tree.

A child without a choice

was chosen to come into this world

with no voice,

to say to him don't cry

and

keep your head up high,

for one day you will understand

why...

Do You?

Do You Think Of Me

Do You Think Of Me When You Pray

Do I Cross Your Mind Any Day

Do You Think Of Me?

Do You Wonder If I'm Okay

Do You Worry About My Day to Day

Do You Think of Me?

Do You Care If I Sleep At Night

Do You Know If I'm Doing Alright?

Do. You. Think. Of. Me?

Encouragement

Don't be afraid to reach for the stars

Don't be afraid to dream beyond Mars.

I dare you to trust someone you cannot see

Because

You'll be amazed at what you can be.

Although

The test of life may seem hard to pass

Just

Trust your faith from first to last.

Don't be afraid to be who you are

Because

According to his will, you are a superstar.

And

When things get rough, you better not quit, just rest

Awhile,

And Pray A Bit.

Fig Tree Faith

Oh ye of little faith,

There is assurance in his grace.

As clear as you can see my face,

As well should be your view of faith.

To the Naysayer, and Non-believers,

Slackers, and under achievers,

If you looking for a piece of mind,

Trust in Jesus and you will find,

All you need to ease your mind...

I'm Better

He Blessed Me In spite of My Mess

He looked inside and saw my best

I'm Better

I took a swing at life, even though it shot me a curve

I still ended up Much

Better

Than

I

Deserve

I'm Better.

My Friend

In life there are things that make us smile.

In life there are things worthy of going an extra mile

It can be:

A hint of pleasure,

A midst of peace.

A child you touch with a lesson you teach.

But

If I had to do it all over again,

I don't think I could do it

Without

My friend.

You were encouragement when courage was vague,

You were there to comfort me in the midst of the rage.

You're My Friend...

Pick Me Up

When a person is down in the world an ounce of hope is better than a pound of preaching.

One can go weeks with no food, days with no water, but only twenty four hours without hope.

As you go from day to day, plant a seed along the way.

Encourage Someone...

Pray

The other day I heard a little voice say, "Lord I don't know if I can make it another day. I don't know if I can continue to deal with people trying to block my way." In the midst of the little voice I heard the Lord say

Pray.

Pray for peace my child, pray for strength to go on for many miles because through it all you are still my child. I created in you a force to handle the rain, and I gave you tough skin to withstand the pain.

Stand tall my child and hold your head up high, and don't worry for only I know the reasons

Why

Pray...

Thankful

I am thankful for what I have been given in this life.

When I see the hand I could have been dealt, I thank the Lord twice.

So many people are hurting with no way to ease their pain.

Can somebody please tell them, this is just a little Rain?

He that is last, will one day be first, and then one will truly understand the meaning of this verse.

I am thankful for my troubles because I know trouble won't last.

I'm thankful he keeps on blessing me in spite of my past.

I'm thankful for my good days along with the bad.

The truth of the matter I am even thankful when I'm sad.

Some wonder how I do it, and others say oh He won't last.

Before you judge me, you might want to check my past.

I'm Thankful...

The Word

Genesis gave me a revelation that the end was gone come.

It spoke of lies and deception of the evil one.

He walks the land going to and from,

Seeing how many souls he can overcome.

He will never win because Jesus died,

So we all may have a chance to live again.

Stay in the furnace,

And

Know if you trust Jesus

You'll

Come out Untarnished...

To My Brothers On Lockdown

To my brothers on lockdown I know you still pray,

You pray to the Lord for a better day.

A better day is coming is one thing I can say.

Hold on to your faith in spite of what they say.

To my brothers on lockdown I know you still pray,

You pray to erase the things in your past,

Don't worry for even those things won't last.

See

I know you still pray...

Untitled

Love me when I least deserve it because that is when I really need it.

Hate me when I'm at my best, even if I act conceited.

Tolerate me when I'm in pain,

So that I don't remain the same.

Encourage me along the way,

Even if I forget to pray.

Work on Me Jesus...

You Can Do Better

You've done a lot of things, but you can do better.

You took a swing at life, and the bat got heavier.

Still

You can do better.

You lost your way, and your pay.

Still

You can do better.

You are stressed,

Depressed,

And a Mess.

Still

You can do better.

You can do better, I know you can.

You hold the power to defeat

The Man

You Can Do Better.

LIFE

The chapter on life was inspired by events that the author has experienced or seen. Life can be captured in the essence of time. Yesterday is in the tomb of time, but tomorrow is in the womb of time. Once you realize that your life is not determined by the mistakes you have made, but rather by the lives and people that you touch along the way. At that very point is when you truly begin to live life. In life one should appreciate the things he has been given because the outcome could have been far worst. Many people are experiencing hurt with no way to ease their pain however this is just a season or a cycle in life that will make them stronger and better. Accept your troubles and know that troubles don't last. So many people refuse to embrace their struggles that they spend the majority of their life trying to avoid the very test that was designed to make them stronger. When a person feels down in life, an ounce of hope is better than a pound of preaching. Understand that in life you can always do better, even if you accomplish a lot of things, still you can do better. When you are stressed, depressed, and a mess know that this is just a phase, and it too shall past. As things get rough, as they sometimes will, stay in the furnace because it's all just a drill. It is my desire that this section helps someone to appreciate the struggles that have made them the person they are today.

Am I

Am I that rock that's been your distraction?

Am I the one that's impaired your attraction to reach for better things?

Am I that enabler that hindered your from reaching your full potential, your inner destiny, your earthly aptitude?

Am I the cause of:

Your downfall;

Your doubt;

Your distraction;

Your demise?

Am I?

If this is the case, and it just might be, you're better off without me...

Are You Damaged Goods?

I understand that marriage number one was a mistake, but you rushed into marriage number two right after your first date.

You won't last if you keep going at this rate

A heart is strong, but just like a bone,

with too much pressure it will break.

Find your wings, and free yourself,

for only you can determine

your true wealth.

But

I really don't understand what happen to you. You were once in the top percent of your class, now you seem so desperate searching for love that won't last.

Hey

If you decide to marry again,

make sure this time it's a

friend

You Might Be Damaged Goods...

Don't Trust Them

Mass media pollutes the majority of all nations,

Masked in hidden conversations of what's best for you.

Have you ever noticed that everything that is good, ends up being bad?

And we are the ones left holding the bag?

Do you know what's really true, do you know who really looks out for you?

Taxation without representation still exists today, and the only thing that has changed is your rate of pay...

Don't Trust Them...

It's In My Blood Line

I am addicted to struggles, but I love the Fame.

I'm not afraid of a challenge it's just a little rain.

I'm content with my life, yet I yearn for change.

Things are bound to get better they just can't remain the same.

Judas betrayed Jesus and we all see the price.

Imagine how things would be if Judas had remained quiet like mice.

No need to worry

No Need to fear

Tell my enemy there is no victory here

It's In My Blood Line

Lesson

I'm so glad my Mother raised me on

Black eyed Peas,

Collard Greens,

Candy Yams,

And

Lima Beans,

She gave me food that made me smart,

She gave me food cooked from the heart.

I'm glad my mother raised me to be the man I am today.

I'm glad my Mother taught me to

Pray.

Lost

Like a needle in a hay stack

or

salt in the sand.

There is something trapped inside this man.

I try, and I try, to do all that I can,

but

needless to say

I'm only the next

man.

If I am the head,

then where is the

tail.

Can we honestly say

that justice

prevails.

I'm lost...

My Testimony

I've had some struggles, but I won't complain.

I've been in the storm, but I survived the rain.
I've lost some people along the way.

There have been times when all I could do was pray.

I buried my mom, and my dad.

Seems like I lost the only friends I ever had.

I've had some struggles, but I won't complain.

There has been some joy in the midst of this rain.

We all have a story that needs to be told.

I'm still in the fire, waiting to come out pure gold.

I've had some struggles, but I won't complain.

I've been in the storm, but I survived the rain.

My Testimony

No Parole

Life can seem so long to the living,

but

yet so short to the dead.

The majority of my existence occurred only in my head.

When the time was right,

I gave no fight,

I exposed myself with all thy

might.

How could something so right

end up so wrong, as if it were the

words of a sad, sad love song.

As I sit incarcerated within these walls,

I wonder will I ever mount up

like a cannon ball.

No Parole...

No Surface

For years, months, weeks, days, and hours the same struggle oppresses

thee.

After dying a million times over, I finally realize death only occurs within

me.

If I am too powerful to be penetrated,

or too unique to be duplicated.

Then why is my life so complicated?

Have I been trained to resist

or

Do I resist to be trained.

For years, months, weeks, days, and hours I've been afraid to come from
under the shower.

I can't surface...

Partly Cloudy

I've reached a new height in my elevation, and now I see clearer now.

So many protest this storm that I'm facing, but to me it's like floating on air.

Without a care, without a concern, my body is transcending in an element of time,

I

Don't

Want

To

Come

Down.

What if we could reach the stars, tweet to mars, and communicate with outer beings?

Smile

I'm tripping right,

Remember

I'm

Partly Cloudy...

Random Thoughts

If I told you my untold story of all my sad days

Could you handle it?

If I told you all my broke times, when I didn't have a dime

Could you handle it?

If I told you I've almost lost my mind, many times

Could you handle it?

I Just did...

Could you handle it?

Repent

Forgive me Father for I have sinned.

I did it over and over again.

You think I'd learn from my mistakes.

I guess I wanted to see how much you would take.

I am thankful for what I have, but yet I want more.

I have seen so many blessings just sitting at my front door.

I know the Kingdom can be mine, If only I can stay Faithful during tough times.

I come to you as Humble as I know how.

Eliminate temptation so that I might completely do the will.

For I know

When it's all said and done,

This Was Just A Drill...

The American Dream

How can a dream be controlled by so many,

How can a dream rely on the fate of others?

How did the dream skip me,

my sisters,

and,

my brothers.

Is it a curse passed down by our mothers?

or

Is it a plot to oppress

all

Brothers?

They told us to read, and they change the books,

they told us to be professional,

so

We changed our looks.

To remedy it all,

Maybe they would rather

we just cook.

The American Dream...

The Truth

The toils of life press me down, but I'll never show it.

I've had Fame in the Midst of Rain, and all I did was blow it.

I've been to the Valley and the Mountain Top, but why does it feel like my life is in a Box.

I'm Stressed, Depressed, and a Mess, and you would never know it.

I've drank tears for water, when I didn't have a dime, but when you looked at me, you said oh, he's doing just fine.

To most I appear to be on top of my game, but the truth of the matter is I am the farthest away from fame.

How do I do it? Is the question you ask? I say I did it with Jesus, for only he knows the struggles of my task.

The Truth.

We Use To Be

We use to be friends,

but now we are foes.

That is just the way life goes.

Seasons change,

People come and go,

but you always go back to what you know.

We Use To Be...

REGRET

The chapter on Regret was inspired by the poem, "The Day After." After writing this poem I realized that on this journey called life there will be many things that you regret. It's okay to regret things in life, as long as you are able to forgive yourself, and others. All of the pieces in this section didn't directly happen to me, but to those that I have had the pleasure of knowing. Sometimes during regretful situations we feel that a veil could not hide the pain we feel inside, and we truly feel as though we are a victim of a suicide. Often times when we are faced with situations that we know are a bit risky. We go against the grain, and all that exists in our brains, for just a moment, is fame. We know in our hearts that it's all just game, but we allow ourselves to be blinded by the fame. In order to move on from this situation, one must allow himself time to heal the hurt and the pain that goes along with the encounter with fame. Once this happens the healing process can take place. I created an exercise where I listed all the things I love, and all the things I regret. In my findings I found out that I love way more than I regret. I truly hope this section helps someone to forgive some of the encounters that have taken place in their life.

Betrayed

I gave you my heart time after time.

I shared my wealth down to the last dime.

How could you do it, I thought we were friends.

I guess there was a motive behind that silly grin.

If I had to do it all over again, I probably wouldn't choose you as my friend.

I can forgive you because it's the Christian way,

But the next time you need a friend, do me a favor and just don't come my way.

Judas betrayed Jesus and we all see the price.

Now you understand why I am as quiet as mice

I've been Betrayed.

The Day After

A cloak could not begin to hide

The Pain I felt inside

For allowing myself to

be a victim of a

Self-homicide.

I went against the grain,

and all that existed in

my Brain

and traded years of sanity,

for a moment with

fame.

Why could I not recognize the game,

why was I blinded by the fame.

I knew better than to think that it was different from the rest,

Even if this experience was better than my best.

But only time can heal the hurt and the pain

That comes along with my encounter with fame.

I got played

Can You See It?

It's invisible to the naked eye

Yet Powerful enough to make you cry.

No one knows the pain it brings

It's colder than winter, and warmer than spring.

It starts out a secret

but

Ends up a lie

I wish I could kiss this nightmare goodbye.

So foolish to think it couldn't happen to me, the strongest link on the family tree.

Can you see it?

I Didn't Listen

Tis was the night before spring break when you broke my heart,

Right after we maxed out my American Express Card.

A decade has passed and I still can't forget

The very first time we shared a

Kiss.

I still have visions of sugar plumes dancing in my head,

Memories of you relaxing in my bed.

I promised myself, I would move on,

but I can't get over the fact that you are gone.

You got a hold on me that just won't end

I can't seem to forget your girlish grin.

I was told to be careful from the start

Somebody Shouted

She's got your heart!

I didn't listen...

I'm Numb

It's just not the same,

I know it's hard to accept, and I can only imagine your pain.

I'm Numb

And

We must move on.

I know you think about what used to be,

but

Baby it's gone.

The truth of the matter is I wish you would move on.

I'm Numb...

Patterns Don't Change

As I look around I see seasons gone

and

Seasons prolonged.

I realize now what they felt then,

When I quoted the words

when oh when.

If respect is what was sought,

then why is it no longer being taught.

Whatever became of our traditions, have they too been forgotten

along with the conditions.

If I am the captain of this ship,

then why am I still shackled at the hip.

Patterns don't Change...

Pickle Juice

The taste of life can be bitter and sweet

making you cautious of every person you

meet.

It's hard to believe the things we feel

When we know deep in our minds

They could never be real.

An image of hope it starts out to be,

Only to realize it's a deep dark

fantasy.

Say what you mean,

and mean what you

say.

Pick up the pieces,

Then kneel and pray.

Pleasure

Pleasure has principles, pleasure has pain.

Some places pleasure can be found can be considered strange.

Pleasure

If used out of context

Can

Be

A

Dangerous

Thing.

Pleasure.

Sacred

How can something so powerful

be taken so lightly.

If one truly knew the value it would

be kept so tightly.

The power to give,

The power to receive,

If used incorrectly an easy target

for greed.

It's a gift from our maker that makes us unique.

It's powerful enough to cause one to lose sleep.

Some tag it with emotions,

Some use it as potions,

Others allow it to be the center of commotion.

Do we blame it on Adam

or

Can we blame it on Eve.

Do they carry the burden engulfed by greed.

Is it sacred..?

LOVE

This chapter on Love was inspired by the poem "Unity". There is more to life than loving yourself; you have got to take the time to love someone else. Many people spend a life time holding love hostage, but once it is released they begin to gain self-worth. Love can be the very essence of life. Love can really be a beautiful thing, but finding love can sometimes be a dream. I was always told that if you work at something long enough, it will surely harvest in front of you. For some, they have accepted the terms that love won't come for them however, there is still more to life than loving yourself, you have got to take the time to love someone else. Yesterday is a thing of the past, which means that you can't focus on the past bad experiences you have encountered with love. Tomorrow is in the developing stages, and there is always a chance that you might find love. If you do obtain love, remember to give love a chance. There are people who look down their family tree and see the absence of love like a generational curse. Take a woman for example, mother was without love, her mother was without love, and now the daughter is without love. Same holds true for a man, father was without love, his father without love, and now the son is without love. There is a life motto that I always adhere to: If you always do, what you have always done, you will always get what you always gotten. If your mother couldn't find love then it is time to change. If your father couldn't find love, and you find yourself in the same boat as your father, then it is time to change. No change, No gain. Finally, we all must search for love until we find that one person that blows our mind. I hope that this chapter serves as an eye opener for someone searching for love.

Woman

A gift, a Woman is the reason a man stands. He stands through the test and toils of life in hopes of one day finding a wife.

A wife to love, a wife to hold, a wife worth more than her weight in gold.

A Woman is a unique as can be, but what more could you expect it's a gift from him to me.

Me being Man, her biggest fan, to love, and to keep until life suffers a defeat.

I love you this day, and the rest of my life, and I'm glad Woman was created to be Man's

Wife.

A Lovely Lady

A Lovely Lady is what you are

A perfect creation by far.

The nicest thing I ever imagined

Oh how one would love to be

Your magic dragon.

A mere example of God's gift to man

You possess the power to understand.

The message that's hidden between the words

Of the two little humming birds.

Tweet, Tweet, Tweet goes the song

I hope the music plays until dawn.

And we spend forever in each other's

Arms.

A Lovely Lady...

A Second Look

When I first saw you, you didn't catch my eye.

As time progressed you grew on me.

Now my days are filled with thoughts of you.

Hoping that one day they all will come true.

You are addicted to work, and we can never spend time, but it's always fulfilling when one of us drops a dime.

You jokingly say that you will stop working if I take care of you, if only you realized that I am trying to make that come true.

I don't care about your expensive taste, I don't even care about the money you waste.

I'm captivated by you, since I took that second

Look...

Family

Some we like,

Some we love,

Some we overlook just because they mean so much to us.

They make us fuss,

They make us curse,

They even cause our cheeks to blush.

But we love them all just the same,

We battle the storms,

and

We survive the rain.

We're Family and that's enough

We stick together when times are tough.

We lean and depend on each other,

And we do what we can for our sisters and brothers.

We're Family what else can we say,

But

Watch over us, as we go from day to day.

Family

I Miss You

All A Brother Wants Is To Have You Back In His Life.

If I Get a Second Chance, I'll make You My Wife.

I Can Still Smell Your Perfume, As If You Just Left The Room.

My Heart Is Hurting, It's filled with

Gloom.

All A Brother Wants Is To Have You Back In His Life.

I Promise You This Time I Won't Lose You Twice.

I Miss Your Smile

Your Warm Embrace

I Even Miss The Shadow Of Your Face.

I Miss You!

Misunderstood Love

Lullabies of loneliness, dry tears of emptiness,

I can't see, hear, or touch you.

Help me feel you.

But

You said you loved me, then you left me, I never knew that was love.

You left me alone in this dark, cold world, you were my sun, my light, my warmth.

Your words comforted me, protected me, and made me wiser.

Please come back!

I can't make it on my own, I'm too weak,

I need you, I love you!

I get it…

You loved me more.

So Be It…

My Bad

It's funny, I met you through another friend, and we have stood the test of time.

I can honestly say that you are truly a friend of

Mines.

I know I missed the BBQ that you threw me, and I even missed your daughter birthday,

But

When it's all said and done, we are still friends at the end of the day.

You are in my top ten....

My Brother From Another

For almost two decades we have been brothers, always taking the time to uplift each other.

I will always remember the lessons that we have shared, the times we laughed, and showed each other we cared.

When March 19th comes around, you'll always get a call, even if I'm not in town.

Everyone needs a role model to kind of pave the way, and you have been that model every step of the way.

Thanks..

My Brother from Another....

Question

Is it better to love someone that doesn't love you back?

or

Love someone who belongs to the Brother across the tracks.

What can I truly gain from a love like this, a life time of misery, and a life that is an uncertain bliss?

But

What do I do to remedy this pain because I know that things can't remain the same?

I guess all I can do is hope for the day, a special someone comes my way.

Question

The Essence OF Love

Love is what you make it, as long as you can take it, it's the very essence of life.

Many spend a life time searching for love, never finding that true someone to peak that urge.

When you find that special someone that curves your thirst for love, embrace the very essence of them.

Understand that in a twinkle of an eye, this love could die never to exist again...

The One That Got Away

Not a day goes by that I don't think about the time when we were together.

It's funny because we both thought we would be together forever.

I remember the day we met, you gave me a smile that I'll never forget.

I miss our conversations, and how we expressed ourselves with no limitations.

If I could turn back the hands of time, I know you would be mine.

I am sorry for all the pain I caused, I should have been more of a man, and showed some balls.

The One That Got Away...

To My Surprise

I met an Angel the other day, and he truly helped me along the way. He never spoke of religious things, and his greatest concern was for my

Well-being.

I wonder why this Angel came my way, we spent countless hours, talking about my day to day.

My encounter with this Angel was the strangest thing that had ever happen to me.

After my encounter with this Angel,

Now I truly feel free...

Unity

There is more to life than loving yourself; you have got to take the time to love someone else.

Love can really be a beautiful thing, but finding love is sometimes a dream.

There is more to life than loving yourself, you got to take time to love someone else.

Yesterday is in the tomb of time

But

Tomorrow is in the womb of time.

Search for love until you find

The one person that blows your mind

Unity